ANCIENT WISDOM
LIVING TRADITION

For John,
thank you
for supporting
Clear Light Direct

Marcia Keegan

ANCIENT WISDOM
LIVING TRADITION

The Spirit of Tibet in the Himalayas

Marcia Keegan

Translated from the Tibetan by

Lobsang Lhalungpa

With additional translations by
Geshe Tashi Gyaltsen and Glenn H. Mullin

Foreword by
His Holiness The Dalai Lama

Clear Light Publishers
Santa Fe, New Mexico

© 1998 Clear Light Publishers
Photographs © 1998 Marcia Keegan
Translations © Lobsang Lhalungpa, Geshe Tashi Gyaltsen, and Glenn H. Mullin

Clear Light Publishers
823 Don Diego, Santa Fe, NM 87501

First Edition
10 9 8 7 6 5 4 3 2 1

Library of Congress Cataloging-in-Publication Data

Keegan, Marcia
    Ancient wisdom, living tradition : the Tibetan spirit in the Himalayas / Marcia Keegan ;
        edited and translated by Lobsang Lhalungpa.
            p. cm.
        ISBN 0-940666-75-8
        1. Buddhism—Quotations, maxims, etc. I. Lhalungpa, Lobsang
    Phuntshok, 1926-   II. Title
    BQ135.A53   1997
    294.3—DC20   96-41271
                                                      CIP

Printed and bound in Hong Kong, China by Book Art Inc., Toronto

Front Cover: Lama Pema Choegen

THE DALAI LAMA

Foreword

When Tibet was first unified under the rule of the early kings, it was a military force to be reckoned with. Tibetan influence extended from Mongolia in the north, to the banks of the River Ganges in the south. In due course, the nature of this influence changed. Tibetans gradually evolved a peaceful culture, in which compassion, contentment and wisdom were predominant values. Two major factors contributed to this transformation. One, of course, was the introduction of Buddhism, largely from India, with its discipline of restraint from harming others, its great aspiration towards enlightenment in order to help all beings and its refined view of reality. The other was Tibet's vast, uncrowded and unspoiled environment. The clear open sky, rolling plains and soaring mountains were conducive to the spirit of freedom that came to characterize the Tibetan way of life.

Tibet exercised a strong attraction for its neighbours. The great monastic institutions became centers of education and culture. Huge libraries of books were collected. Meditation practitioners developed an intimate understanding of the workings of the mind. Physicians refined a unique science of medicine. Society as a whole treated the natural environment and the animals with whom they shared it with respect. Students from the surrounding Mongolian and Himalayan regions were warmly welcomed and took what they had learned back to their own lands.

Today, despite the wanton destruction of so much that we held dear in Tibet, I believe that Tibetan culture continues to have much to contribute to the world at large. This is confirmed by the great interest that people living in the regions bordering Tibet and further afield continue to show in things Tibetan. Marcia Keegan, who has long been a friend of Tibetans and a fervent supporter of our cause, has sought in this book to convey a vivid impression of her own experience of the inspiring qualities of Tibetan life. I am sure that readers will share my gratitude to her, and those who have helped her, for the dedication they have brought to their work.

Introduction

The Buddha was born in India in the 6th Century BC, and over the succeeding centuries his teachings transformed much of Asia. Though it continued to thrive elsewhere, by 1000 AD, Buddhism was disappearing from the land of its origin.

The great realization of the Buddha's Enlightenment is beyond conceptualization, yet the Buddha taught with words, sometimes with gesture or action, often with a story. As Buddhism spread across Asia, indigenous cultures mingled their own colors in the various streams of Buddhist expression, creating unique art, sculpture and architecture; vast bodies of literature and commentary; music, dance and theater.

The Buddhist culture that I personally am most attracted to, and that I have portrayed in this book, is that which was formed in the highest, most inaccessible place in the world—the Himalayan plateau. Today this Buddhism is under attack in Tibet, where it is being sustained at great cost by a people not yet ready to give up their uniqueness. Outside Tibet, along its borders, Tibetan Buddhism endures in the culturally related nations of Bhutan and Nepal and in parts of India that include Sikkim, Ladakh and the various Tibetan refugee settlements.

Mahayana or "Great Vehicle" Buddhism—the Buddhism of Northern Asia—was introduced to Tibet beginning in the 7th Century. A century later, the sage Padmasambhava founded the country's first Buddhist monastery and did much to further Tibet's conversion to the new religion. Tibetans were transformed from a warrior-like mountain folk to gentle monks, farmers and tradesmen. Tibetans melded their own artistic traditions with the inspirations of Buddhism, creating a unique and colorful tradition of painting and sculpture. The new monasteries were built in distinctively Tibetan style and guarded by mythic creatures from both Buddhist and local legend. Buddhist holidays were celebrated with community-wide festivals, at which monks performed music, dance and drama, or lampooned the mighty and poked fun at absurd human foibles—proving that even boisterous folk comedies could fit comfortably into ritual Buddhist life. Eventually social customs, legal and governmental structures were completely informed by Buddhist beliefs.

While the sutras—the words of the Buddha—were memorized, copied and repeated from generation to generation of Himalayan monks, great meditators and teachers wrote poems and essays of commentary on those teachings. The insights of the Indian and Tibetan masters were also passed down through the ages, forming a living body of wisdom held in trust by the great monastic communities sheltering in valleys and clinging to the rugged mountains.

The Buddha's words were the core of an ever-growing body of literature, expanding like crystals around a diamond. A Tibetan Buddhist seeking inspiration might look to the *Dharmapada*, a collection of sayings of the Buddha. Or she might consult the teachings of Shantideva, an Indian Sage of the eleventh century—or turn to the writings of Tibetan monastics that range from Lama Mipham Namgyal to the Seventh Dalai Lama. Many stanzas of these texts were common sayings in Tibet, as

quotations of Shakespeare and the Bible are in the West. The stanzas that appear in this book are drawn from all these sources: the words of the Buddha; the writings of a classic Indian Buddhist master; and the poetry and teachings of Tibetan sages and scholars. New translations were made for this book by the Tibetan scholar Lobsang Lhalungpa and by Geshe Tashi Gyaltsen, and Glenn H. Mullin was kind enough to allow us to reprint some of his translations.

Until the Chinese invasion in 1949, the heart of Tibetan culture lay at the capital city, Lhasa. At the peak of Tibet's power, its influence was felt from China through Mongolia all the way to the borders of India and Afghanistan. Though its political influence shrank as Tibet's armies dwindled and its people exchanged their swords for prayer wheels, even up until 1959 the living arteries of trade routes carried a constant flow of cultural exchange between Tibet and its sister Himalayan countries of Bhutan, Sikkim, and Ladakh, and the regions of Nepal settled by people of Tibetan descent.

Then, in 1959, when the Chinese violently secured their control of Tibet and began the horrific slaughter of monks and nuns and the demolishing of Tibet's monasteries, the vibrancy of Buddhism in Tibet was extinguished. The Dalai Lama fled to India, beginning an exodus that

would sweep hundreds of thousands of Tibetans into exile. Those who could not or did not escape suffered terribly: Out of a population of 6 million Tibetans, around 1.2 million have lost their lives; many more have suffered imprisonment and torture. Buddhist worship is restricted; Tibetan language and arts are no longer taught in schools; and as the Chinese population swelled through state-sponsored immigration, Tibetans have become impoverished second-class citizens in their own country.

With the Chinese Occupation and the Dalai Lama's exile, the heart of Tibetan Buddhism has been cut out of Tibet and transplanted further south, in India. In part because India has been so hospitable to the Tibetan refugees, Buddhism once again has a strong presence in the land of its birth. Tibetan Buddhist refugee settlements are scattered from the Himalayan foothills in India's north to the jungles of the south in Karnataka state. The flow of Buddhist ideas now links Indian towns like Dharamsala, the Dalai Lama's current residence, with traditional Tibetan Buddhist communities in Sikkim and Ladakh (now part of India), and with communities in Nepal, where recent Tibetan refugees have joined Tibetan settlements of long duration. Newly refurbished monasteries in Outer Mongolia are revitalizing that country's Tibetan Buddhist tradition. From this reorganized nexus of Tibetan Buddhism, the great teachings once hidden behind towering mountain peaks are now disseminating across the world, taught in Western universities and available on the Internet.

My long-time study of Buddhism led to the opportunity to meet His Holiness the Dalai Lama on his first visit to the United States and Canada, in 1979. I had the good fortune to be able to follow and photograph his tour, attending and recording many lectures and conversations, and to publish a book, *The Dalai Lama's Historic Journey to North America*, as a result of that experience. The connection with His Holiness was—and is—a blessing of a magnitude that is impossible to describe.

In the course of time, I was also able to travel to many of these countries where Himalayan-style Buddhism is still flourishing—India (including Sikkim and Ladakh), Bhutan and Nepal. On these travels I met lamas, scholars and lay people who sustain the living Buddhist tradition. I took teachings and visited monasteries, saw shrines and sacred pilgrimage sites. Everywhere, I enjoyed the hospitality and warmth of the people who live in these regions. Since I had had many opportunities to photograph the Dalai Lama, I usually carried some of my photographs with me in order to give them to people that wanted them. It still brings tears to my eyes to remember the joy of monks in Ladakh, eagerly receiving and immediately framing and installing on their altar a portrait of the Dalai Lama.

In 1986 I was able to visit Tibet for the first time. Since it was not so dangerous to do so then, I hid away a large cache of photos of the Dalai Lama to give away. Everywhere I met people who seemed to crave that photo more than any other thing I could have offered them.

In Tibet I visited those few religious sites preserved (like the Jokhang) or restored for the tourist trade. But I spent much more time touring the shattered monasteries outside Lhasa, with their defaced frescoes and decapitated Buddha statues. Among the bomb-blasted rubble were burned scraps of ancient texts, the incinerated remains of a thousand years' meditative insights.

Terrified monks escorted me, pointing out the devastation, whispering of bombs and death. I could only imagine the bloodshed, torture and violence that ended the monastic lives of so many of those who had once taken sanctuary here among the sangha, the Buddhist community.

When we could escape from the ever-present Chinese escorts, I would give my new friends that dangerous but precious treasure they craved—the Dalai Lama's portrait.

The Dalai Lama's was not the only portrait I took to Tibet. In the early 1980s I studied with a Tibetan monk who later became the Ganden Tripa, the appointed head of the Gelugpa order. By the time he received this appointment he had been living in India with the refugee community for some time, but the Gelug monks still in Tibet were proud to claim this noted scholar and tantric master as their leader, and he was especially

revered at Ganden, the monastery that is the traditional seat of the Ganden Tripa. I visited this monastery, or what was left of it, bringing his picture with me as a gift for the remaining Ganden monks.

Ganden was destroyed by the Chinese during the cultural revolution. Though parts of the monastery have since been reconstructed, it was still rubble when I was there. The vast spaces were almost deserted, and I laid my heavy camera bag down on a stone as I wandered through the rooms that once housed over 7,000 monks. In the silence, I tried to envision the bustle of monastic and collegiate activity that once enlivened the place.

Turning a corner, I was startled to see a picture of Ganden Tri Rinpoche lovingly placed on an improvised altar in one slightly more intact room. I went closer. To my surprise, it was my own photo of Rinpoche. How could this be? My picture was safely in the camera bag. Then I remembered: I had given some copies of the picture to Ganden Tri Rinpoche himself in India. The only explanation possible was that one of his friends had somehow smuggled the picture into Tibet. Ganden Tri Rinpoche, though appointed by the Dalai Lama to his official position long after he and many other Ganden monks had fled to India, had travelled back to Tibet by proxy, in this photo. To those few monks of Ganden who survived and kept the tradition in Tibet, he was present as their leader as surely as if he still lived among them.

Some of the photos I carried with me I had made at a Kalachakra initiation given by the Dalai Lama in Bodhgaya, India. This particular initiation is one of the most profound and complete for monks and laity alike, and its sanctity was intensified by the fact that it was celebrated at Bodhgaya, the holy site where the Buddha attained enlightenment.

At the time, for an ordinary Tibetan to travel to India was all but impossible, but there were a number of Tibetans who were determined not to miss this once-in-a-lifetime event. Among the thousands of people from all over the globe who attended this auspicious Kalachakra were some Tibetans who, at great risk, slipped out of their country into India just for the occasion. Once the Kalachakra was over, many of them secretly slipped back into Tibet, because they feared if they stayed in India, their relatives or friends would be imprisoned by the Chinese as punishment.

I was to encounter one of these daring and determined people, later, in Tibet. At the Potala in Lhasa, feeling rather confident because I was visiting without Chinese escort, I gave copies of the Dalai Lama's photographs to some monks. The photo was one I had taken at the Kalachakra in Bodhgaya, and one monk suddenly said, "I was there! I saw you take that photograph."

Our encounter seemed fated. "I took that picture so I could give it to you today," I said to him. Suddenly, a chill fell over our group as we became aware we were not alone. A Chinese soldier I hadn't noticed was at my elbow.

"Do you have another copy of that picture?" the soldier asked. "Please give me one."

I wavered. To my amazement, the soldier seemed sincere. But Tibetans who were accompanying me said, "Don't give it to him—he's Chinese, and he might use it to cause trouble." Their argument was certainly persuasive, yet I was still uncertain.

I asked myself, "What would the Dalai Lama do in such a situation?" It seemed that an answer came to me—that it would be right to give a copy of the picture to the Chinese soldier. I did, and he received it with a rush of gratitude and many bows—all of which, of course, could have been a sham. And then the soldier disappeared into another room. I couldn't restrain my curiosity, and tiptoed after him a few moments later. I came to an open door and glanced inside. Alone in the room, the soldier was holding the photo of the Dalai Lama to his heart, sobbing. Tears were streaming down his face. My own eyes were misting over as I hastily tiptoed away.

I still have no explanation for this unusual event, but I know that the daring monk from the Potala and I were very fortunate that day, encountering a Chinese soldier who was so mysteriously sympathetic. It reminded me that even in a situation where strong divisions between "enemy" and "friend" exist—such as in occupied Tibet—things are never as simple as they seem. A tenet of Buddhism is that our enemy is our greatest teacher, and here the lesson was that sometimes the enemy may be revealed as a secret friend. Tibet has need of many such secret friends.

Travelling in Tibet in 1985, I was aware it was risky to give out photos of the Dalai Lama, but the Chinese had not yet focussed as much repressive attention on this "act of subversion" as they do now. Travellers today are advised not to try to take His Holiness' pictures with them or to give them to Tibetans, as those who receive them are put in grave danger. I also understand that it is now much harder to get to and photograph the vandalized and destroyed temples that I saw. Today Chinese tour guides escort the traveller to monasteries and temples that have been partially restored, but the many more utterly ruined ones are off-limits.

Those who led me to the destroyed temples, and those whose joy in owning a photo of the Dalai Lama shines so visibly out of the photo I took years ago, have no doubt changed significantly in their appearance by now. I would have not wanted to publish these photos immediately, for fear of endangering those Tibetans shown here, but so much time has passed that the people are almost certainly no longer identifiable.

I hope that their continued yearning for the freedom of their country, and for the return of their beloved spiritual leader the Dalai Lama has not since led them into danger, imprisonment or death. If they still survive, they survive as second class citizens in a police state that monitors and crushes their every move toward religious, social and political freedom.

Tibetan Buddhism may be thriving in the diaspora beyond Tibet, but those who live in Tibet today are cut off from its lifestream, like limbs amputated from a living body. How much longer can they survive in repression and isolation?

As I cherish the images of Tibetan Buddhist culture and wisdom, art and learning that still grace the rest of the Himalayan region, I pray that freedom—the freedom of religious belief and worship, the freedom to speak their own language, follow their own customs, and determine the future of their own country—will one day return to the land which gave birth to this gorgeous and profound tradition.

Marcia Keegan

Monks holding pictures of the Dalai Lama in Tibet

What is the crown jewel
That effortlessly fulfills all wishes?
The Supreme Mahayana teacher
Who guides one along a perfect path.

Songs of Spiritual Change
The Seventh Dalai Lama

His Holiness performing the Kalachakra in Bodhgaya

Just as mountains and rocks
Are unshaken by the wind,
Those who are wise
Are unmoved by praise or abuse.

The Dhammapada (Pali)
Sayings of the Buddha

Himalayas

Rumtek Monastery, Sikkim

I rejoice in the happiness of all beings, in their virtuous deeds,
And in the alleviation of suffering of all tormented realms.
I rejoice in accumulating virtuous deeds, the causes of enlightenment;
I rejoice in the liberation achieved by sentient beings.

The Sevenfold Devotion
Traditional

Stick together in happiness and misery
Like a bunch of ears of grain.

On Good Conduct
Dujom J. Yeshey Dorje

Festival in Hemis, Ladakh

Jokhang

Why crave the searing flame
Of sensual enjoyment and racing thoughts?
Why not rather seek
The lamp that illumines the darkness?

Dharmapada (Sanskrit)
The Concise Words of Buddha

Tibetan farmer

Tree in Darjeeling

A person who is not arrogant but calm
Who is a delightful companion and reliable friend
Is like a good tree laden with fruit.
Anyone sitting under its delightful shade will gain solace.

The Tree Poem
Gungthang Jampalyang

Roof of the Jokhang Temple

One must never disturb the joy of one's mind!
Holding on to distress will not
Help fulfill one's wishes.
Indeed, it will undermine one's virtues.

Bodhisattvacharyavatara
Shantideva

29

Rinpong Monastery, Paro, Bhutan

All accumulated wealth is eventually dispersed;
What goes up must come down.
All meetings end in partings;
Every life concludes in death.

The Dharmapada (Sanskrit)
The Concise Words of Buddha

Little Jokhang

All things that appear in the world are
Seen as an inconceivable abode of wisdom,
And the endless beings dwelling therein
Are known to be an ocean of Buddhas.

Songs of Spiritual Change
The Seventh Dalai Lama

Suffering has good effects,
Sorrow helps clear arrogance.
Feel sympathy for the existential wanderers:
Let go harmful deeds and delight in virtuous ones.

Bodhisattvacharyavatara
Shantideva

Tibetan elder in Lhasa

Paro Taktsang in Bhutan

Night is long for a watchman.
Distance is long for a tired traveler.
Existence is long for a person
Who is ignorant of the Dharma.

The Dharmapada (Sanskrit)
The Concise Words of Buddha

Yumba Lakhar in Tibet

Rumtek Monastery in Sikkim

Regard the body as a vessel,
A vehicle for journeying to and fro.
Treat it as a wish-fulfilling body
For benefitting all sentient beings.

Thus, while securing one's personal freedom,
Show always a smiling face,
Banishing frown and flattery,
And develop honest friendships with other sentient beings.

Bodhisattvacharyavatara
Shantideva

Tibetan woman in Lhasa

Potala in Tibet

By gaining control over the mind, they achieved liberation
From inner bondage and contamination, and won perfect freedom.
The Enlightened and Compassionate Ones have transcended attachment
They watch over sentient beings in the universe in order to help them.

The Dharmapada (Sanskrit)
The Concise Words of Buddha

Sikkim landscape

Buddha in Kathmandu

The benefit of ruling over all the earth,
The benefit of being reborn in Paradise,
And the benefit of having dominion over the universe,
Are all inferior to the benefit of entering the path of
Enlightenment.

The Dhammapada (Pali)
Sayings of the Buddha

Elder paying homage to the Potala in Tibet

One who is just and judicious
Emulates the great qualities of others.
He is like a gentle stream in a fresh meadow,
Whisking away flower petals as it purls softly along.

The Water Poem
Gungthang Jampalyang

Geshe Gyatso at Ganden Monastery in Tibet

Kyichu River in Tibet

It's easy to see the good and bad qualities of others
But difficult to perceive one's own faults.
A lake clearly reflects the moon and the stars
But cannot mirror its own depth.

The Water Poem
Gungthang Jampalyang

With reverent gesture I entreat
The Buddhas in all pure realms
To light the lamp of Dharma
For all sentient beings.

Bodhisattvacharyavatara
Shantideva

Making offering at Bakna Lubuk cave

Yamdo Yutso

Just as water flows through your fingers,
Let go of any evil thought.
Just like grasping a rock,
Firmly hold every virtuous thought.

The Regal Code of Conduct
Mipham Jamyang Namgyal

So many boys and girls
Die young—
Why believe that youth
Is any protection against death?

The Dharmapada (Sanskrit)
The Concise Words of Buddha

Farmer in Bhutan

Some people say
"I have sons as well as wealth."
Since there is no self inside or out,
Whose sons and wealth are they?

The Dharmapada (Sanskrit)
The Concise Words of Buddha

Family traveling in Tibet

From the moment of entering his mother's womb,
A sentient being never remains still
But moves along through passage after passage
Without ever returning.

The Dharmapada (Sanskrit)
The Concise Words of Buddha

What is the great ocean
Most difficult to leave forever?
The ocean of samsara's three worlds,
Which tosses in waves of suffering.

Songs of Spiritual Change
The Seventh Dalai Lama

Temple fresco depicting planetary diagram in Paro, Bhutan

Roof of the Potala in Tibet

If the "elephant mind" is controlled,
Bound with the rope of mindfulness,
There won't be any danger
And all virtues will flow into one's hand.

Bodhisattvacharyavatara
Shantideva

Deer dance in Bhutan

One who has tamed his passions,
Renouncing pride and destroying negative emotions—
He is like a wild horse
That has been tamed by the skilled horseman.

The Dhammapada (Pali)
Sayings of the Buddha

A leisurely and blessed life is exceedingly hard to find.
When one has found an opportunity to serve humanity
And fails to devote oneself to helping others,
How can one find it again?

Bodhisattvacharyavatara
Shantideva

Sera monk in Tibet

Ganden Monastery in Tibet

There is no wealth equal to generosity;
There is no eye equal to wisdom;
There is no friend equal to learning the Dharma;
There is no ornament equal to noble qualities.

The Regal Code of Conduct
Mipham Jamyang Namgyal

Spinning prayer wheel at Drepung Monastery in Tibet

Jokhang

You are the lamp
That lights the Path
And eliminates the darkness of ignorance

The Dhammapada (Pali)
Sayings of the Buddha

The perfume of flowers floats on the wind
Like the aroma of incense and sandalwood.
But the scent of holiness is never dispersed,
For the essence of the Buddha is all-pervasive

The Dharmapada (Sanskrit)
The Concise Words of Buddha

Wild flowers in southern Tibet

Yaks in Tibet

May I be a wishfulfilling gem,
Powerful prayers and healing balm;
May I become like a wish-granting tree
And a cow of plenty for all sentient beings.

Bodhisattvacharyavatara
Shantideva

Bhutanese dancer

Waterfall in Bhutan

Just as a turbulent river
Rushes ever onward,
So human life passes
Without ever returning.

The Dharmapada (Sanskrit)
The Concise Words of Buddha

Leh Palace in Ladakh

Even though words do not have sharpness,
They cut the heart into pieces.
Even though the wind does not have wings,
It fills space with whirlwind.

Ancient oral wisdom
Traditional

This day my life is fruitful,
My human life a blessing;
This day am I
The child of Buddha.

Bodhisattvacharyavatara
Shantideva

The wise one's mind is quiet.
So also his speech and deeds.
Insight has made him free
And all his actions sublime.

The Dhammapada (Pali)
Sayings of the Buddha

Monk in Rumtek Monastery in Sikkim

Monk blowing conch, Spituk Monastery, Ladakh

Matho Monastery in Ladakh

The world of man abounds
With evil and great sickness.
Through the true gift of loving kindness,
These are purified.

The Dharmapada (Sanskrit)
The Concise Words of Buddha

The young monk who devotes himself to the Teachings,
Shows the correct path to the people,
And eliminates the darkness of ignorance
Is like the moon sailing free from the clouds.

The Dhammapada (Pali)
Sayings of the Buddha

Lama Pema Choegen

Himalayas

Nowhere in the sky
Nor in the ocean
Nor in a cleft of the mountains,
Is there an earthly place
Where one may make a stand
And vanquish death.

The Dhammapada (Pali)
Sayings of the Buddha

Spituk Monastery in Ladakh

Geshe Tashi Gyaltsen lighting offerings

The greatest blessing is health;
Contentment is the truest wealth.
The spiritual friend is one's dearest relative,
Enlightenment is the ultimate bliss.

The Dhammapada (Pali)
Sayings of the Buddha

Making offering at Jokhang

His Holiness the Dalai Lama, Kalachakra, Bodhgaya

Everybody turns to someone
Who is compassionate and generous
The way merchant ships constantly return
To the harbor of a treasure-laden sea.

The Water Poem
Gungthang Jampalyang

Padmasambhava in Potala

Mural in Ladakh

Mural outside Lhasa

Painting mural, Tikse Monastery, Ladakh

If someone acts with wisdom
He or she can do anything!
If the highest Buddhahood can be achieved,
Then there is nothing that cannot be accomplished.

The Regal Code of Conduct
Mipham Jamyang Namgyal

Virtuous and vile deeds have this in common:
They both fill the mind little by little
Like raindrops accumulating and rising
To form a large pool of water.

The Water Poem

Gungthang Jampalyang

Prayer flags in Darjeeling

Mani stones in Bhutan

Chortens in Ladakh

Just as a silversmith
Turns rough ore into sterling,
So does a wise person
Steadily purify his inner contaminations.

The Dharmapada (Sanskrit)
The Concise Words of Buddha

Bestow upon me the transforming powers to see
Every living being as my own parent
And, in order that I may eradicate suffering,
Help me to know the ways of the wise.

Songs of Spiritual Change
The Seventh Dalai Lama

Pilgrim in Ladakh

This Bodhicitta is the best ambrosia
For destroying the lord of death.
It is an inexhaustible treasure
To eliminate the poverty of sentient beings.

It is the best medicine
To cure the diseases of sentient beings.
It is a great tree that relieves
The exhaustion of wandering beings.

It is a bridge that helps
Sentient beings cross the lower realms.
It is a rising moon of the mind
That cools the scorching heat of emotions in sentient beings.
It is the great sun
That illuminates the dark ignorance of sentient beings
It is the creamy butter that emerges
Through the churning of the milk of dharma.

Bodhisattvacharyavatara
Shantideva

Bhutanese herder

Every timely action will bring results
Without difficulty.
Every untimely endeavor will fail
If the moment is premature or if the right moment is missed.

The Tree Poem
Gungthang Jampalyang

Near Ganden Monastery, Tibet

102

Not tossed by the vagaries of wicked friends
Or stirred by sudden impulses,
A calm person is like a majestic mountain
Who will dwarf the King of Mountains.

The Regal Code of Conduct
Mipham Jamyang Namgyal

Himalayas

With reverent gesture I implore
Those Buddhas who intend to pass into Nirvana
Not to leave sentient beings in darkness,
But to remain active for countless eons.

Bodhisattvacharyavatara
Shantideva

Padmasambhava festival in Hemis Monastery

Initiate in Kalachakra, Bodhgaya

Even if you do not know the Dharma completely,
Learning a little is beneficial;
Even without drinking the entire river,
You can quench your thirst.

The Water Poem
Gungthang Jampalyang

Ganden Tri Rinpoche, Kalachakra, Bodhgaya

May I become a protector of all helpless beings;
May I become a guide for travelers,
May I become a ship to those wishing to cross the ocean;
May I become a raft and a bridge.

Bodhisattvacharyavatara
Shantideva

Kalachakra thangka

The sand mandala is a geometric diagram symbolizing a
divinity and his or her abode. It is created in order to
invite the divinity's presence, usually to empower and
sanctify a ritual. As a reminder of impermanence, the
sand mandala is destroyed after the ritual's conclusion.

Understanding impermanence
Is the true path to
Inner peace and freedom.

The Dharmapada (Sanskrit)
The Concise Words of Buddha

Kalachakra Initiation, Bodhgaya, India

May the sublime, joyous teachings thrive;
May the lineage holders live long;
And may living beings endless as space
Be moved to attain enlightenment.

Songs of Spiritual Change
The Seventh Dalai Lama

LONG LIFE PRAYER FOR
HIS HOLINESS THE DALAI LAMA

From the three deepest levels of the countless Buddhas
Emerged their multiple emanations,
Performing illusory dances to tame sentient beings
All you gracious lamas, our personal and preceeding lineage,
Who are the Wish-fulfilling Jewels,
The source of virtues and enlightenment,
We invoke you with intense devotion,
So that Tenzin Gyatso, Protector of the Great Land of Snows,
May live for a hundred aeons,
Pour on Him your blessings
That His aspirations may be fulfilled.

To the ocean of the Guardians of the Teaching, who possess the eye of transcendental wisdom
Carrying on their matted locks the knot
Symbolic of the vows they made to the Vajradhara Buddha,
The powerful ones who protect the Teaching and the upholders of the Dharma
We offer you our prayers with intense devotion
That Tenzin Gyatso, Protector of the Great Land of Snows,
May live for a hundred aeons,
Pour on Him your blessings
That His aspirations may be fulfilled.

To all you guileless Ones, in whom we take the excellent Refuge,
We pray with intense devotion, humbly, from our very heart
That, by the strength of these verses,
Ngawang Lobsang Tenzin Gyatso, He who has power over speech,
The kindly One, Upholder of the Dharma, the Great Ocean,
He who possesses the Three Secret Powers, may be indestructible, eternal and without end,
That, seated on the supreme unconquerable Throne of the Vajra,
He may live for a hundred aeons.
Pour on Him your blessings
That His aspirations may be fulfilled.

You who bear the burdens of innumerable Buddhas,
With courage carrying on your shoulders the vast activities of the Fully Enlightened Ones
Working for the good of all beings, like the Wish-Fulfilling Gem,
The Jewel of Jewels,
May your aspirations be perfectly fulfilled.

By virtue of this may the Golden Era be opened
Like a gate to the great Spaces, liberating all sentient beings,
Coming as the happiness of Spring which comforts our sorrows
And helps the Teaching of the Buddha to spread in all directions and in all ages,
Making it prosper to the summit of Samsara and Nirvana.

Oh You with the lotus in Your hand, may the nectar stream of your blessings
Strengthen our mind and bring it to maturity
May we be able to please you by practicing the Dharma.
Through accomplishing at all times the good deeds of the Bodhisattvas,
May we reach Nirvana.

By the blessings of the wondrous Buddhas and Bodhisattvas,
By the unassailable truth of the spiritual laws of cause and effect,
By the unstained power of the pure mind
May the aim of our prayers soon be accomplished.

ཨོཾ་སྭ་སྟི། །རབ་འབྱམས་རྒྱལ་བའི་གསང་གསུམ་
མ་ལུས་པ། །ཀུན་འདུལ་ཅིར་ཡང་འཆར་བའི་རྩེ་འཕྱུལ་
གར། །སྤྱོད་ཅིང་དགེའི་ལེགས་ཀུན་འབྱུང་ཡིན་བཞིན་ནོར། །
དངོས་བཀྱུད་དོན་ཅན་ལྷ་མའི་ཚོགས་རྣམས་ལ། །བདག་
ཅག་གདུང་ཕྱགས་དྲག་པོས་གསོལ་འདེབས་ན། །གདངས་
ཅན་མགོན་པོ་བསྟན་འཛིན་རྒྱ་མཚོ་ཡི། །སྐུ་ཚེ་མི་ཤིགས་
བསྐལ་བཀྱུར་རབ་བརྟན་ཅིང་། །བཞེད་དོན་སྤྲུན་གྱིས་
འགྲུབ་པར་བྱིན་གྱིས་རློབས། །ཆོས་དབྱིངས་ཀུན་གསལ་
ཕྲིན་དང་མཚམ་འཇུག་པའི། །ཧྱུལ་བྱལ་བའི་ཞིད་ཡེ་ཤེས་
སྐུ་མའི་སྤྲུལ། །གངས་མེད་རྗེན་དང་བདེན་པའི་དགྱིས་དགོད་
དུ། །བྱང་བའི་ཡེ་ནས་སྩ་ཚོགས་གྲུམས་ཅད་ལ། །
བདག་ཅག་གདུང་ཕྱགས་དྲག་པོས་གསོལ་འདེབས་ན། །
གདངས་ཅན་མགོན་པོ་བསྟན་འཛིན་རྒྱ་མཚོ་ཡི། །སྐུ་ཚེ་མི་
ཤིགས་བསྐལ་བཀྱུར་རབ་བརྟན་ཅིང་། །བཞེད་དོན་སྤྲུན་
གྱིས་འགྲུབ་པར་བྱིན་གྱིས་རློབས། །ཁྱབ་བདག་དཱོགས་ལོན་དུན་
སྐུན་དྲོགས་པོ་ལས་ཀྱི། །སྣང་བ་འགྲོ་ཁམས་རྒྱ་མཚོར་
དྲག་ཅེན་པས། །ཕན་མཛད་སྤྲོབས་བཀྲ་མའང་ན་ལྟ་ཡི་
ཇྱེ། །རབ་འབྱམས་དུས་གསུམ་རྒྱལ་བ་ཐམས་ཅད་ལ། །
བདག་ཅག་གདུང་ཕྱགས་དྲག་པོས་གསོལ་འདེབས་ན། །
གངས་ཅན་མགོན་པོ་བསྟན་འཛིན་རྒྱ་མཚོ་ཡི། །སྐུ་ཚེ་མི་
ཤིགས་བསྐལ་བཀྱུར་རབ་བརྟན་ཅིང་། །བཞེད་དོན་སྤྲུན་
གྱིས་འགྲུབ་པར་བྱིན་གྱིས་རློབས། །འཛིག་རྟེན་གསུམ་
ལས་གང་གིས་དེས་སྐྱོབ་ཞིང་། །མཆོག་དུ་ཞི་བ་རྣམ་གྲུང་
ཕོར་བྲུའི་གདེར། །ཧྲག་མེན་མི་གཡོ་ཀུན་བཟང་དགོ་བའི་
དཔལ། །ཕྱག་གསུམ་དུས་པའི་ཚོགས་ཀྱི་ཚོགས་རྣམས་ལ། །
བདག་ཅག་གདུང་ཕྱགས་དྲག་པོས་གསོལ་འདེབས་ན། །
གངས་ཅན་མགོན་པོ་བསྟན་འཛིན་རྒྱ་མཚོ་ཡི། །སྐུ་ཚེ་མི་
ཤིགས་བསྐལ་བཀྱུར་རབ་བརྟན་ཅིང་། །བཞེད་དོན་སྤྲུན་
གྱིས་འགྲུབ་པར་བྱིན་གྱིས་རློབས། །སྤྲེད་པའི་འཕྲུལ་
འཁོར་འཇོགས་ལ་ཆེས་དཔའ་བ་འི། །བདེན་དོན་མཛེན་
ཧྲུམ་འཛིན་པའི་ཡེ་ཤེས་ཅན། །རྣམ་པར་རྟོ་རྗེའི་གྲོང་ལས་
མི་ཕྱེད་པ། །རིག་གྱོལ་འཕགས་པའི་དགེ་འདུན་ཕམས་
ཅན་ལ། །བདག་ཅག་གདུང་ཕྱགས་དྲག་པོས་གསོལ་
འདེབས་ན། །གངས་ཅན་མགོན་པོ་བསྟན་འཛིན་རྒྱ་མཚོ་
ཡི། །སྐུ་ཚེ་མི་ཤིགས་བསྐལ་བཀྱུར་རབ་བརྟན་ཅིང་། །
བཞེད་དོན་སྤྲུན་གྱིས་འགྲུབ་པར་བྱིན་གྱིས་རློབས། །མཁའ་

སྤྱོད་ཞིང་དང་གནས་ཡུལ་དུར་ཁྲོད་དུ། །བདེ་སྟོང་ཅ༹མས་
བཀྱུར་རོལ་པའི་རྩེན་འཆོ་ཡི། །རྣལ་འབྱོར་ལམ་བཟང་
སྒྲུབ་ལ་གྲོགས་མཛད་པའི། །ཁནས་གསུམ་དཔའ་བོ་
མཁའ་འགྲོའི་ཚོགས་རྣམས་ལ། །བདག་ཅག་གདུང་ཕྱགས་
ཕུགས་དྲག་པོས་གསོལ་འདེབས་ན། །གངས་ཅན་མགོན་
པོ་བསྟན་འཛིན་རྒྱ་མཚོ་ཡི། །སྐུ་ཚེ་མི་ཤིགས་བསྐལ་བཀྱུར་
རབ་བརྟན་ཅིང་། །བཞེད་དོན་སྤྲུན་གྱིས་འགྲུབ་པར་བྱིན་
གྱིས་རློབས། །རྡོ་རྗེ་འཆང་གི་བཀའ་དཔས་ཕྱག་ཀྱུའི་
མདུད། །མི་འབྲལ་རལ་པའི་གྲོང་དུ་ཅེར་བཀོད་ནས། །
བསྲུན་དང་བསྲུན་འཛིན་སྟོང་པའི་མཕུ་ཐུལ་ཅན། །ཡེ་ཤེས་
སྤྲུན་ལྷན་བསྲུང་སྲུང་རྒྱ་མཚོ་ལ། །བདག་ཅག་གདུང་ཕྱགས་
དྲག་པོས་གསོལ་འདེབས་ན། །གངས་ཅན་མགོན་པོ་བསྟན་
འཛིན་རྒྱ་མཚོ་ཡི། །སྐུ་ཚེ་མི་ཤིགས་བསྐལ་བཀྱུར་རབ་
བརྟན་ཅིང་། །བཞེད་དོན་སྤྲུན་གྱིས་འགྲུབ་པར་བྱིན་གྱིས་
རློབས། །དི་ལྟར་སྐུ་མེད་སྐུབས་ཀྱི་མཆོག་རྣམས་ལ། །འཁྲུ་
དྲག་སྤྲིང་ནས་གུས་པས་གསོལ་བཏབ་མཐུས། །མི་བཟད་
སྐྱགས་མའི་ཆུག་ཏུས་རབ་མནར་བའི། །བདག་སོ་གང་གས་
ལྷོངས་འགྲོ་བའི་མགོན་གཅིག་པུ། །ངག་དབང་རྩོ་བཟང་
བསྟན་འཛིན་རྒྱ་མཚོ་མཆོག །གསང་གསུམ་མི་ཤིགས་
མི་འགྱུར་མ་ནུབ་པར། །ཁཞིམ་གཞིག་ཡངས་པལ་རྟོ་
རྗེ་སྟེ་པ་ངི་ཁྲིར། །བསྐལ་པ་རྗེ་བཞིན་མཚོར་ཀུས་སེན་དྲག །
བདུན་གོག །རབ་འབྱིས་རྒྱལ་བ་ཀུན་གྱི་མཛད་པའི་འཁུར། །
སྟིང་སྟོབས་ཕུག་པར་བཟུང་བའི་རྣབས་ཆེན་གྱི། །ཕྱིན་
ལས་ཀུན་ཁབ་ནོར་བུ་ཧེ་སྟིང་པོ་ཐུ། །བཞིན་པ་ཧེ་བཞིན་
སྐུན་གྱིས་འགྲུབ་གྱུར་ཅིག །དེའི་མཐུན་རྟོགས་ལྷུན་
སྐལ་བཟང་ནས་མཁའི་ཁི། །ལུས་ཅན་འལ་བསོ་དེ་དཔྱེ་
དུ་ཐུག་གྱོལ་ཞིང་། །ཐུབ་བསྟན་ཕོགས་དུས་ཀུན་དུ་རབ་
དར་བའི། །དགེ་མཚན་སྲིད་ཞིའི་ཅེ་མོར་རྒྱས་གྱུར་ཅིག །
ཕུག་ན་འབྲུ་ཡི་བྱིན་རླབས་བདུད་རྗེའི་རྒྱུན། །བདག་སོཧ་
སྟིང་གི་ཅུཔས་སུ་དྲག་སྨྱིན་ཅིང་། །བཀའ་དབཞིན་སྒྲུབ་པའི་
མཚོ་པས་རབ་བསྐྱེན་ནས། །ཀུན་བཟང་སྟོང་མཚོག་རྒྱ་
མཚོ་མཐར་སོན་ཧོག །སྐྱད་ཕྱུ་སྲས་བཅས་རྒྱལ་བའི་
ཕྱིན་རློབས་དང་། །རྟེན་འབྲེལ་སྣ་མེད་པའི་བདེན་པ་
དང་། །བདག་གི་ལྷག་བསམ་དག་པའི་མཐུ་སྟོབས་ཀྱིས། །
སྨོན་པའི་དོན་ཀུན་བདེ་བླག་འགྲུབ་གྱུར་ཅིག །

117

ACKNOWLEDGMENTS

Lobsang Lhalungpa generously provided the majority of the translations from Tibetan for this book, including many stanzas drawn from full-length poems that he has translated. His translations appear on pages 18, 21, 22, 25, 27, 29, 31, 34, 37, 38, 40, 44, 47, 48, 51, 52, 54, 56, 61, 64, 66, 70, 75, 77, 83, 88, 90, 93, 94, 97, 101, 102, 106, 109, 110, and 116.

Geshe Tashi Gyaltsen also helpfully provided translations from Tibetan. The stanzas he translated appear on pages 42, 62, 69, 73, 78, 84, and 86. Geshe Tashi Gyaltsen is an ordained monk and served as assistant to Ganden Tri Rinpoche for fifteen years. He earned his geshe degree in 1995 and serves as a member of the Tibetan parliament and is a member of Ganden Jangtse Monastery.

In addition, Glenn H. Mullin kindly gave his permission to use translations from his book *Songs of Spiritual Change* (Gabriel/Snow Lion, Ithaca, New York, 1982). These quoted stanzas appear on pages 16, 33, 59, 98, 115 and 116. Glenn H. Mullin has chronicled the lives of a number of former Dalai Lamas. He is internationally recognized as a scholar of Tibetan Buddhism.

Valerie Shepherd provided invaluable assistance and expertise in preparation of the text.

TEXT SELECTIONS

The Bodhisattvacharyavatara
by Shantideva

"The Bodhisattvacharyavatara," or "Guide to the Bodhisattva's Way of Life," is a long poem by the eighth-century Indian master Shantideva. Shantideva lived and taught at Nalanda, the great Buddhist university in northern India. Translations from this text were made for the book by Lobsang Lhalungpa and by Geshe Tashi Gyaltsen.

The Dhammapada (Pali) and *The Dharmapada (Sanskrit)*
Teachings of the Buddha

The Dhammapada (Pali) and *The Dharmapada* (Sanskrit) are two separate compilations of verses drawn from the teachings of the Buddha. *The Dhammapada* was written down in Pali, the language of Buddhism in Ceylon, Burma and Indochina. The compilation that is best known in Tibet was translated from Sanskrit, the classic language of India, and is also called the "Concise Words of Buddha." In both Northern (Mahayana) and Southern (Theravada) Buddhism these texts are among the most popular and best known of the entire Buddhist canon. The contents of both collections overlap but are not identical. The Pali and Sanskrit versions of this text each contain verses that do not appear in the other volume. Translations for this book were provided by Lobsang Lhalungpa and Geshe Tashi Gyaltsen.

On Good Conduct
by Dujom J. Yeshey Dorje

Dujom J. Yeshey Dorje was a twentieth-century Nyingma monk who escaped from Tibet and lived in India until his recent death. The poem was translated by Lobsang Lhalungpa for this book.

The Regal Code of Conduct
by Mipham Jamyang Namgyal

"The Regal Code of Conduct," a poem by the nineteenth-century Tibetan master Mipham Jamyang Namgyal, was translated by Lobsang Lhalungpa especially for this book. Mipham Jamyang Namgyal, also called Mipham Jamyang Namgyal Gyatso (1846-1912), was born in Kham, in Eastern Tibet. A great teacher of the Nyingmapa Order, he was an incomparable master of the Buddhist scriptures, literature, poetry, Sanskrit, ancient sciences and arts.

Songs of Spiritual Change
by Gyalwa Kalzang Gyatso

The Seventh Dalai Lama, Gyalwa Kalzang Gyatso, was a prolific and gifted poet. A collection of his poetry, written in the eighteenth century and entitled *Songs of Spiritual Change*, has been translated by Glenn H. Mullin and published by Gabriel/Snow Lion, 1982, New York.

The Water Poem and *The Tree Poem*
by Gungthang Jampalyang

"The Water Poem" and "The Tree Poem" were translated by Lobsang Lhalungpa for this book. Gungthang Jampalyang, also called Gungthang Konchok Tenpai Donmey (1762-1824), was a great teacher and highly attained master of the Gelukpa order from the Amdo Province of Eastern Tibet.